MW01196586

Creating a
Wildflower Meadow

Henry W. Art

CONTENTS

Introduction

Whether your backyard is the size of a postage stamp or the 40 acres in "the back 40," wildflowers can enhance its beauty and add to your enjoyment. This bulletin describes how to grow meadow wildflowers that like plenty of sun and can fill either large or small yards with a seasonal procession of colors. You may desire to convert a portion of the lawn to which you have been enslaved into a beautiful natural landscape. Wildflower meadows cost less than lawns to maintain, and consume much less water, gasoline, fertilizer, and time. On the other hand, you may wish to introduce some native species into existing gardens to supplement your familiar border and bedding plants. In either case, wildflowers can be established with modest invest-ments of time in planning, preparation, properly selected seeds, and patience.

In addition to providing low-maintenance landscaping, wildflowers are extremely versatile. If portions of your yard are too dry or too wet for the usual lawn grasses, certain wildflowers mixed with native grasses may be a beautiful solution to the problem. Many of the species in this bulletin (such as black-eyed Susan, butterfly weed, and purple coneflower) will attract butterflies to your garden. Scarlet sage and standing cypress, with their bright red flowers, are pollinated by hummingbirds. These species and others (such as gayfeather, blanketflower, and wild bergamot) make excellent cut flowers as well.

Selecting Wildflowers

The wildflowers I suggest you consider have been selected because they are native to North America, reasonably easy to grow, and are well behaved once established. Although some of these wildflowers are native only to a specific region, all of them can be grown over a wide range of environmental conditions in other regions as well. There are many other species that could easily be added to your backyard and you might want to consult *A Garden of Wildflowers, The Wildflower Gardener's Guide,* or other references listed on page 30 for further suggestions.

When I use the term "wildflower" I am referring to species of plants that can grow on their own with little or no attention from the gardener. Weeds are one form of wildflower, but are not recommended in this bulletin. While some species such as ox-eye daisy and chicory may be attractive, they also may become aggressive and take over your backyard. The following is a short list of alien (non-native) wildflower species that should be avoided for that reason.

Alien Wildflower Species

African daisy	Four-o'clock
Baby's breath	Foxglove
Bachelor's button	Ox-eye daisy
Bouncing Bet	Purple loosestrife
Candytuft	Queen Anne's lace
Chicory	St. John's-wort
Corn poppy	Silene
Cornflower	Sweet alyssum
Dame's rocket	White yarrow

For best results, the wildflowers you choose should be compatible with the environmental conditions typical to your region. The list of wildflowers on page 4 is keyed to the regional map on page 5, and can be used as a general guide for the selection of wildflowers. More information about these wildflowers appears on pages 16–29.

WILDFLOWERS BY REGION

Common Name	Scientific Name	NE	MW	SE	GP	RM	SW	NW
Annual phlox	*Phlox drummondii*	X	X	X	X	X	X	X
Baby blue-eyes	*Nemophila menziesii*	X	X	X	X	X	X	X
*Black-eyed Susan	*Rudbeckia hirta*	X	X	X	X	X	X	X
Blanketflower	*Gaillardia aristata*	X	X	X	X	X	X	X
Blue flax	*Linum lewisii*	X	X	X	X	X	X	X
Blue-eyed grass	*Sisyrinchium bellum*						X	X
Butterfly weed	*Asclepias tuberosa*	X	X	X	X	X	X	X
California poppy	*Eschscholzia californica*	X	X	X	X	X	X	X
Chinese houses	*Collinsia heterophylla*		X	X		X	X	X
Colorado columbine	*Aquilegia caerulea*					X	X	X
Cosmos	*Cosmos bipinnatus*	X	X	X	X	X	X	X
*Eastern columbine	*Aguilegia canadensis*	X	X	X	X	X		X
Farewell-to-spring	*Clarkia amoena*			X		X	X	X
*Gayfeather	*Liatris pycnostachya*	X	X	X	X	X	X	
Lance-leaved coreopsis	*Coreopsis lanceolata*	X	X	X	X	X	X	X
Linanthus	*Linanthus grandiflorus*					X	X	X
Mexican hat	*Ratibida columnifera*		X	X	X	X	X	
*New England aster	*Aster novae-angliae*	X	X	X	X	X		X
Pasqueflower	*Anemone patens*	X	X		X	X		X
*Purple coneflower	*Echinacea purpurea*	X	X	X	X	X		X
Scarlet sage	*Salvia coccinea*			X	X		X	X
Spiderwort	*Tradescantia virginiana*	X	X	X		X		X
Standing cypress	*Ipomopsis rubra*	X	X	X	X		X	X
Tidy tips	*Layia platglossa*					X	X	X
Wild bergamot	*Monarda fistulosa*	X	X	X	X	X		
Wind poppy	*Stylomecon heterophylla*						X	X
		NE	MW	SE	GP	RM	SW	NW

*requires cold treatment for germination of seeds

Wildflower & Grass Region Map

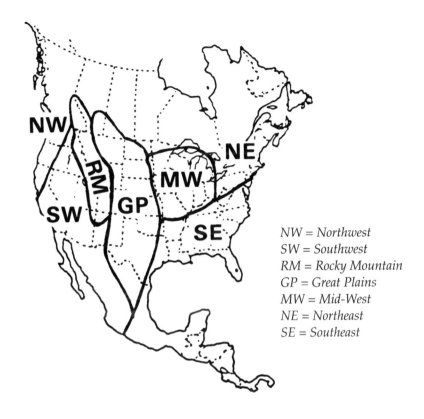

NW = Northwest
SW = Southwest
RM = Rocky Mountain
GP = Great Plains
MW = Mid-West
NE = Northeast
SE = Southeast

Some wildflowers are "hardy" and tolerate freezing temperatures, while others are "tender" and are killed by frosts. Take your local climate into consideration when selecting wildflowers, remembering that sunny southern slopes are usually warmer, and shady northern slopes may be substantially cooler, than the average climate of a region. For example, if you live in a northern region you may be able to grow more southerly wildflowers on south-facing, protected slopes.

You will probably want to plant several different species of wildflowers, drawn from a rich palette of complementary colors and giving a seasonal succession of bloom. To help you make your choices, the tables on pages 6 and 7 arrange the wildflowers by color and by season of flowering.

Color

Species	White	Pink	Red	Orange	Yellow	Blue	Purple	Lavender
Linanthus	X							
Cosmos	X	X	X					
Colorado columbine	X					X		
Pasqueflower	X					X	X	
Farewell-to-spring		X	X					
Eastern columbine		X	X		X			
Annual phlox		X	X				X	
Scarlet sage			X					
Standing cypress			X					
Wind poppy			X	X				
Blanketflower			X	X	X			
Mexican hat			X		X			
Purple coneflower			X					X
Black-eyed Susan				X	X			
Butterfly weed				X				
California poppy				X				
Lance-leaved coreopsis					X			
Tidy tips					X			
Blue flax						X		
Baby blue-eyes						X		
Blue-eyed grass					X	X		
Spiderwort						X	X	X
Chinese houses						X	X	X
New England aster							X	
Wild bergamot								X
Gayfeather								X

Flowering Progression

Species	E Sp	M Sp	L Sp	E S	S	L S	E F	F
Pasqueflower	X							
Baby blue-eyes	X	X						
Blue-eyed grass	X	X						
Wind poppy		X						
Chinese houses		X	X	X				
Tidy tips		X	X	X				
Eastern columbine		X	X	X	X			
Linanthus		X	X	X	X			
Spiderwort		X	X	X	X			
Farewell-to-spring			X	X				
Annual phlox		X	X	X	X	X		
Lance-leaved coreopsis			X	X	X			
Colorado columbine			X	X	X			
Butterfly weed				X	X			
Wild bergamot				X	X			
Standing cypress					X			
Blue flax					X			
California poppy	X	X	X	X	X	X	X	X
Cosmos			X	X	X	X	X	
Mexican hat			X	X	X	X	X	
Purple coneflower				X	X	X	X	
Black-eyed Susan			X	X	X	X		
Scarlet sage			X	X	X	X	X	X
Gayfeather					X	X	X	X
Blanketflower					X	X	X	X
New England aster						X	X	X
	E Sp	M Sp	L Sp	E S	S	L S	E F	F

Key: **E Sp** — Early Spring **M Sp** — Mid-Spring **L Sp** — Late Spring **E S** — Early Summer **S** — Summer **L S** — Late Summer **E F** — Early Fall **F** — Fall

How to Obtain Wildflowers

Wildflowers should never be dug from the wild except as part of a rescue operation to save plants that would otherwise be destroyed. Wildflowers are usually propagated either by making cuttings and divisions or by planting seeds. There are a growing number of reputable wildflower propagators who grow their own stock rather than digging plants from the wild. Many of these suppliers will take phone and mail order requests for wildflowers. However, live plants are quite expensive, perhaps prohibitively so if you intend to plant a large area.

By far the least expensive means of growing wildflowers is from seed. The quickest way to obtain wildflower seeds is to purchase them from a reputable supplier. Seeds are generally available year-round and can easily be sent through the mail. If you are planning to plant large areas, you should inquire about wholesale prices for wildflower and native grass seeds. The names of several suppliers are listed on page 31, but their inclusion on the list is by no means an endorsement. The names of other seed companies can be obtained from your nearest native plant society, botanical garden, or U.S. Department of Agriculture Extension Service agent.

Use caution before using prepared wildflower seed mixtures. Although some suppliers will carefully formulate mixes especially for your region using high-quality native species, others simply add the cheapest, most readily available seeds regardless of their desirability. If you are going to spend your money on wildflower seeds, you might as well purchase species that will survive well in your region and not *pay* for roadside weedy wildflowers (such as those listed on page 3) that you wouldn't want in your backyard. So find out what is in the mixture of wildflower seed before you buy the can or packet.

By far the most pleasant way to obtain wildflower seeds is to collect them from the wild. If you collect seeds, remember to follow common sense conservation guidelines. Collect a few seeds or fruits from each of many plants and *only from common species that are locally abundant.* Be careful not to trample nearby plants while you are collecting. Do not collect fruits and seeds from plants growing in public places, and be sure to obtain permission from property owners before you collect on private property.

One of the most satisfactory ways to collect small seeds from wildflowers is to wait until the flowers start to wilt and then to make a small bag out of nylon stocking. Gently place a section of stocking over the developing fruits, and tie both ends using twist-ties, being careful not to crush the stem. When the fruits are fully ripe and dry, simply snip the stem and place the nylon bag into a paper sack.

It is best to separate the seeds from the dried remains of the fruit. Place the collected material on sheets of heavy white paper and gently crush the dried fruits. Blow gently across the paper to remove most of the unwanted husks and fruit residues, being careful not to blow the seeds away. A kitchen sieve is quite useful for cleaning small seeds. Put the seeds in small coin envelopes or zip-closure bags and store them in a cool, dry place.

Cold Treatments

A few of the wildflowers presented in this bulletin have seeds requiring exposure to cold temperatures in order to germinate. These species are marked with an asterisk (*) on the wildflower list. Typically these are wildflowers from regions with cold winters and have evolved this protection to prevent their seeds from germinating in the autumn only to have the tender seedlings killed by frost. However, most of these wildflowers can be grown successfully even in regions with mild winters if the seeds are first given an artificial cold treatment. Once established, these wildflowers will produce flowers and seeds, but the new seeds will not germinate unless they also receive cold treatments.

If you live in a region with cold winters, it is best to plant the seeds of these wildflowers outdoors in the autumn. If you live in a region with mild winters and want to give these species a try, or if you want to plant the seeds in the spring rather than in the autumn, give them an artificial cold treatment before planting peat moss, place them in a zip-closure bag (labeled in waterproof ink with the name of the species), and put the in the refrigerator for 2–3 months. This treatment will enable the seeds to germinate quickly in the spring. If some of the seeds sprout during the cold treatment, just plant them in the spring, being careful not to disturb their fragile root systems.

Selecting Grasses

Natural meadows and grasslands are a combination of wildflowers and grasses. The grasses provide support and the ideal amount of competition for the wildflowers to grow straight and tall. Without the grasses some of these wildflowers might become scraggly or "leggy." In northern regions the dead remains of the grasses provide additional insulation, protecting the over-wintering roots of the wildflowers.

Not all grasses, however, are the same; different species grow in different ways. Some grasses form "sod," which is ideal for lawns, tennis courts, and putting greens, where a continuous, tight cover is required, but is not much of an environment for growing wildflowers. Other grasses form distinct clumps or "bunches" when they grow, allowing space for wildflowers to coexist. When establishing your wildflower meadow, the grasses you interplant with the wildflowers should be bunch grasses. Avoid planting ryegrasses or bluegrasses, which would form sod turfs and crowd out the wildflowers.

Some grass species grow better in some regions than in others. To help you select grasses suited to your region, the table of suggested species is keyed to the map on page 5. Native wildflower seeds should be combined with a *mixture* of native grasses suited to your region.

Grasses should comprise about 60–90% of the seed mixture. The wildflower and grass seed mixture should be sown at a rate of 5–20 pounds of live seeds per acre, depending on the species composition. If species with small seeds (such as switch-grass and California poppy) make up the bulk of the mixture, the seeding rate should be lower than when the mixture is composed mainly of species with large, heavy seeds (such as northern dropseed and wild bergamot). If you purchase wildflower and grass seed in bulk, the supplier can make specific seeding-rate recommendations, but typically 6–7 pounds of wildflower seeds are mixed with enough grass seeds to sow an acre.

Bunch Grass Suggestions

Common Name	Scientific Name	NE	MW	SE	GP	RM	SW	NW
Big bluestem	*Andropogon gerardii*	X	X	X		X		
Blue grama	*Bouteloua gracilis*		X	X	X	X	X	
Broomsedge	*Andropogon virginicus*	X	X	X	X			
Buffalo grass	*Buchloe dactyloides*		X	X	X	X	X	
California oat grass	*Danthonia californica*					X	X	X
Tufted hair grass	*Deschampsia caespitosa*	X	X	X	X	X	X	X
Indian grass	*Sorghastrum nutans*	X	X	X	X		X	
Indian ricegrass	*Oryzopsis hymenoides*				X	X	X	X
June grass	*Koeleria cristata*		X	X	X	X	X	X
Little bluestem	*Andropogon scoparius*	X	X	X	X	X		
Needlegrass	*Stipa spartea*	X	X	X	X	X	X	X
Northern dropseed	*Sporobolus heterolepsis*	X	X	X	X	X		
Poverty three-awn	*Aristida divaricata*			X	X	X	X	
Sheep fescue	*Festuca ovina*	X	X	X	X	X	X	X
Side oats grama	*Bouteloua curtipendula*	X	X	X	X	X	X	
Silver bluestem	*Bothriochloa saccharoides*			X	X		X	
Switch-grass	*Panicum virgatum*	X	X	X	X		X	
Western wheatgrass	*Agropyron smithii*	X	X	X	X	X	X	X

When to Plant

In general, wildflower seeds germinate in response to ample moisture and warm temperatures, although some seeds require cold treatment before they will respond. Ideally you should plan to plant the wildflower and grass seeds to take advantage of the natural precipitation and temperature patterns of your region. Obviously you would not want to plant a meadow in midsummer, when, in most parts of North America, heat and droughty conditions might make it difficult for seeds to germinate and seedlings to become established. Pay attention to the regional and local climate and plan your planting accordingly. Here are a few suggestions for the various wildflower growing regions:

The Northeast (NE) has ample rainfall throughout the year, with cold winters and mild summers. The best time to plant is in the autumn (October to early November) and the next-best time is in mid-spring (late April to mid-May). The best time to plant most western wildflowers in the Northeast, however, is in the spring.

The Southeast (SE) region also has precipitation that is ample and evenly distributed throughout the year. Summers are hot and humid, and winters are generally mild, though frosts may occur anywhere except on the south coasts of Florida and Texas. The autumn (October and November) is the best time to plant, and in the spring after frost danger has passed is the second choice.

Midwest (MW) has cold winters and hot summers. There is increasing tendency for periodic summer droughts toward the west, where there is generally less precipitation than in the east. The optimum planting time is in the early spring as soon as the ground can be worked (mid-March to late April). Mid-autumn (October and November) is the next-best time to plant.

The Great Plains (GP) stretch from Canada to Texas and have a range in winter temperatures from very frigid to cold. Summer temperatures are generally hot. There tends to be less precipitation here than in the Midwest or Southeast since the Great Plains lie in the rain shadow of the Rocky Mountains. Soil moisture is more plentiful in the spring than in other seasons, so it is best to plant in the late fall, before the ground freezes, to allow the wildflowers and grasses to take full advantage of the natural moisture.

The Rocky Mountains (RM) region typically has cold winters and warm summers with low humidity. Most of the precipitation accumulates in the form of snow during the winter and is released in the spring when most of the wildflowers bloom. The best planting in this region is during the autumn.

The Southwest (SW) is an area of scanty rainfall. In southern coastal California, most of this rain comes during the winter. Summer thunderstorms occur more frequently inland. The summer and early autumn temperatures are frequently in the 90–100°F. range. Winter temperatures range from cold in the north to balmy in the southern portions of California and Arizona. The best time to plant is in the late autumn just before the winter rains start.

The Northwest (NW) has cool winters and mild summers with considerable amounts of rainfall throughout the year, especially during the winter. Whether to plant in the spring or fall depends upon the species of wildflowers and grasses being planted. Spring-flowering wildflowers should generally be planted in the early fall, and autumn-flowering wildflowers should be planted in the spring.

Preparing Bare Ground

The easiest time to create a wildflower meadow is when the land is bare and you do not have to deal with established, competing grasses, weeds, herbaceous plants, or woody seedlings. If you are planting a large area of bare ground it may be easiest to hire a landscaper to disk and then rake the soil surface with tractor-drawn equipment. Smaller areas can be raked by hand. Most of these wildflower and grass species benefit from additions of *rotted* manure, compost, or other appropriate seed-free organic matter along with ground limestone at the time the soil is being prepared.

If time permits, have the ground raked again about three weeks later. The second raking will help kill any weeds that sprouted from seeds brought to the surface by the initial soil preparation. Then plant the wildflower and grass seed mixture. If you cannot plant your meadow until the following planting season, sow a cover crop of buckwheat, oats, or annual rye on the area in the fall, and plow it under as a green manure before sowing the wildflower and grass seeds.

How to Plant Seeds

It is best to sow the wildflower and grass seeds on a windless day, broadcasting them by hand or using a whirlwind seeder. Try to apply the seeds as uniformly as possible over the ground surface. If large areas are to be planted it may be worthwhile hiring a landscaping contractor to use a seed drill to plant them. Hopefully your planting has been timed to take advantage of natural rainfall, but if the rains should fail, keep the soil moist, but not wet, until the seeds have germinated and seedlings start to become established. A light covering of seed-free straw will help conserve moisture and reduce erosion until the meadow is established. Do not use baled field hay, which is likely to contain the seeds of exotic grasses, species you want to prevent from invading your meadow.

Transforming an Existing Field

Instead of bare ground, you are more likely to be confronted with an existing lawn or field that you want to convert to a wildflower meadow. *Resist any impulses to use herbicides or fumigants to kill the existing vegetation.* Herbicides are more likely to create problems for the wildflower enthusiast than solve them. They cause damage to the environment, and are not likely to save you any time in establishing a wildflower meadow.

The least effective way to try to create a wildflower meadow is to simply scatter seeds into an existing lawn or meadow. Most of the seeds won't make it through the existing grass but will be consumed by insects or small mammals. Few of the seeds will germinate and become established. The best way to turn an existing field into a wildflower meadow is to start on a small scale and not tackle the entire back 40 at once.

Two strategies can be deployed in your battle against existing sod: spot seeding and transplanting live plants that you have raised. In either approach you need to carefully prepare the site before planting. It is best to start a year in advance, or at least start in the previous spring for fall planting or in the late summer for spring planting.

As soon as the soil can be worked at the beginning of the growing season, dig up patches of the field, turning them over with a sharp spade or rototiller. The patches should be 3–8 feet in diameter and dug in a random pattern, to create a more natural effect than would result from placing them in straight rows. Remove as many of the existing grass roots as possible, and water the soil to encourage the germination of weed seeds that have been stirred up in the process. Then cover the patch with heavy-gauge black plastic sheet mulch, pieces of discarded carpet, or even thick sections of newspaper. If you do not care for the sight of such coverings, you can spread a layer of bark mulch or soil on top of them. If the covering is thick enough, it will eventually shade out and kill off any remaining grass and the newly germinated weed seedlings. Enough rain will soak through or get under the coverings to keep the ground below moist.

Leave the coverings on the patches throughout the growing season, then remove them at planting time. (If black plastic mulch or carpet sections have been used, it may be possible to use them again to create the next year's patches). Rake the ground surface, and plant the grass and wildflower seeds, gently raking them below the soil surface. Alternatively, the seeds can be mixed with an equal volume of soil and the mixture broadcast in the bare patches.

Instead of planting wildflower seeds in the patches you may wish to transplant live plants. These may be raised in your own nursery beds or in plastic trays with small conical depressions, producing "plugs" of wildflowers. Grass seed can also be planted in small pots to make plugs. If you plant seeds in containers, use a mixture of sand and peat moss as a starter soil. Whether you sow the seeds in beds, flats, or trays, do it at the beginning of the growing season. By the time the patches are prepared, the plants will be ready for transplanting.

Plant the plugs in the patch, spacing the grass clumps 12–15 inches apart, and placing the wildflowers in between them. Alternatively, wildflower plants can be transplanted into the patches, and the grass seed sown around them. In either method, the meadow will benefit from an initial watering and a light mulch of seed-free straw.

If your meadow already has bunch grasses, and you do not care to introduce new grass species, live wildflowers can be planted directly into the field. Clear a small patch about a foot in diameter with a cultivator and pick out the grass roots. Set the wildflowers so the bases of their shoots are at ground level. Press them down firmly so the roots are in good contact with the soil beneath, and water well.

Repeat the steps each year until you are satisfied with your wildflower and native grass meadow. It may be a slow process, but even in nature a beautiful wildflower meadow, resplendent with a great diversity of desirable plants, is rarely produced in a single year.

Wildflower Meadow Maintenance

Once the wildflower meadow is established it is relatively easy to maintain. Mow the meadow once a year with a rotary mower, after the growing season is over and the seeds have set; otherwise the natural process of succession may eventually turn your field into a forest. Woody plants will be clipped off and eventually eliminated by mowing, but grasses and wildflowers will be relatively unaffected.

Meadows, grasslands, and prairies can also be maintained by periodic burning, which kills invading shrub and tree seedlings. Do not burn a meadow until after the second season, but then you can burn it every several years. Meadows are best burned in the dormant season on windless days, when the grass is dry but the soil is still wet and the humidity is sufficiently high to minimize any fire danger to surrounding areas. If the meadow grass is too thin to support the fire, dry straw can be scattered about and ignited. Be careful to observe local, state, and federal regulations concerning outdoor burning, in addition to the usual safety practices. Check with your local fire department about obtaining an outdoor burning permit.

In some suburbs there are ordinances dictating aesthetic standards for landscaping. If you live in such a community you might want to check with city hall before turning your front yard into a prairie. If there are prohibitions, you can always try to change the law to encourage landscaping with native plants. Native plants are rarely the "weeds" that these ordinances are trying to prohibit, and it is unlikely that your black-eyed Susans or wild bergamots are going to march through your neighbor's Kentucky bluegrass.

Species of Wildflowers

Annual Phlox
Phlox drummondii

The common annual phlox listed in many seed catalogs is native to east Texas, where masses of them add brilliant pink, red and purple hues to the spring landscape. Annual phlox is a "winter annual" which blooms in the early spring. Its seeds are dormant until the autumn Texas rains stimulate germination.

COLOR: Pink, red, and purple
FLOWERING: Summer
FRUITING: Summer
HEIGHT: 6–20 inches
GROWTH CYCLE: Annual

Baby Blue-Eyes
Nemophila menziesii

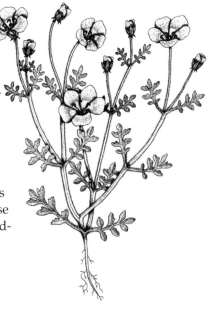

There are several variations on the blue and white theme in this wildflower. The flowers are usually blue at the tip, and white with flecks or radiating streaks of blue at the base. Other forms are all blue, or sky blue with dark blue dots at the base of their petals. Baby blue-eyes flowers open and close in response to air temperature, the petals folding inward at night or in the cold.

COLOR: Blue and white
GROWTH CYCLE: Annual
HEIGHT: 10–20 inches
FRUITING: Spring to early summer
FLOWERING: late winter to early spring

Black-Eyed Susan
Rudbeckia hirta

Black-eyed Susan is a hardy perennial which can be grown as an annual in most locations. The 2–3-inch flower heads, with dark brown centers and yellow or yellow and orange outer petals, are borne on a relatively long stalk, making the black-eyed Susan an attractive cut flower.

COLOR: Yellow and orange
FLOWERING: Summer
FRUITING: Summer to early fall
HEIGHT: 1–3 feet
GROWTH CYCLE: Annual, biennial, or perennial

Blanketflower
Gaillardia aristata

This wildflower blankets parts of the Great Plains with yellow and red daisy-like flowers all summer long. Blanketflower has long been cultivated as a cut flower and was introduced into Europe as a garden plant in the early 1800s.

COLOR: Yellow and red
HEIGHT: 2–4 feet
FLOWERING: Summer to frost
FRUITING: Late summer to fall
GROWTH CYCLE: Hardy perennial

Blue Flax
Linum lewisii

This widely distributed wildflower of the western two-thirds of North America is a relative of the European species from which linen is made. Individual flowers usually last only a day, withering in the hot sun, but new flowers in the cluster bloom each day.

COLOR: Blue
FRUITING: Mid-summer to fall
FLOWERING: Summer
HEIGHT: 1–4 feet
GROWTH CYCLE: Hardy perennial

Blue-Eyed Grass
Sisyrinchium bellum

This wildflower is a member of the iris family, though its flowers don't look much like those of most garden irises. Blue-eyed grass has small, saucer-shaped, purple-blue to lilac flowers. The petals, which open with the sun and close at night and when cloudy, have blunt tips with a projecting point.

COLOR: Purple-blue to lilac
FLOWERING: Early to mid-spring
FRUITING: Late spring
HEIGHT: 6–12 inches
GROWTH CYCLE: Tender perennial

Butterfly Weed
Asclepias tuberosa

The orange, flat-topped clusters of butterfly weed flowers are one of the most striking summer sights in North American prairies. The fused petals of the flower form a crown with 5 projecting horns, which surround masses of sticky pollen. The pollen attaches to the feet of butterflies that visit to drink sweet nectar from the fragrant flowers.

COLOR: Orange
FLOWERING: Late spring
  to summer
FRUITING: Early to mid-fall
HEIGHT: 1–2½ feet
GROWTH CYCLE: Hardy perennial

California Poppy
Eschscholtzia californica

California poppy flowers have a shiny luster to their golden-orange petals, which open in the sunshine and close at night and on cloudy days. Flowers produced early in the spring tend to be larger than those produced later in the season.

COLOR: Golden-orange
FLOWERING: Spring to fall
FRUITING: Late spring to fall
HEIGHT: 1–2 feet
GROWTH CYCLE: Tender perennial, self-seeding and growing as an annual in northern regions

Chinese Houses
Collinsia heterophylla

The common name Chinese houses refers to the whorled pagoda effect of the tiers of blue and white flowers, which encircle the top of this plant's stem. Chinese houses grows nicely in partial shade.

COLOR: Blue and white
FLOWERING: Mid-spring to early summer
FRUITING: Summer
HEIGHT: 1–2 feet
GROWTH CYCLE: Annual

Colorado Columbine
Aquilegia caerulea

The most common variety of Colorado columbine has sky blue and white flowers, while other varieties are all white or all light blue. They are pollinated primarily by hawkmoths and bumblebees, although some bumblebees take a shortcut and consume the nectar without pollinating the flower, by chewing off the knob at the tip of the spur.

COLOR: Blue and white
FLOWERING: Late spring to
   mid-summer
FRUITING: Summer
HEIGHT: 1–2½ feet
GROWTH CYCLE: Hardy perennial

Cosmos
Cosmos bipinnatus

This native of Mexico has found its way further north and into many seed catalogs. Its flower heads are borne atop long stems, a feature which makes cosmos an excellent cut flower.

COLOR: Red, pink or white
FLOWERING: Late spring to
   early fall
FRUITING: Summer to fall
HEIGHT: 3–5 feet
GROWTH CYCLE: Annual, but
   self-seeds even in northern areas

Eastern Columbine
Aquilegia canadensis

The showy, nodding flowers are borne on leafy stems at the top of the plant. The flowers, which may be up to 2 inches across, have 5 spurred, scarlet petals which cover the yellow centers. Bumble-bees pollinate the flowers as they hang upside down to extract the sweet nectar from the spurs.

COLOR: Scarlet and yellow
FLOWERING: Mid-spring to early summer
FRUITING: Summer
HEIGHT: 1–2 feet
GROWTH CYCLE: Hardy perennial

Farewell-to-Spring
Clarkia amoena

This native of California and Oregon, named in honor of Captain William Clark, was introduced into Europe as a garden flower not long after the Lewis and Clark Expedition. Each of the fan-shaped petals has a darker red botch toward its base.

COLOR: Red
FLOWERING: Late spring to early summer
FRUITING: Summer
HEIGHT: 1–3 feet
GROWTH CYCLE: Annual

Gayfeather
Liatris pycnostachya

The graceful lavender spikes of gayfeather sway in the summer winds of the prairies of the U.S. heartland. The opening of the flower heads starts at the top and progresses toward the bottom.

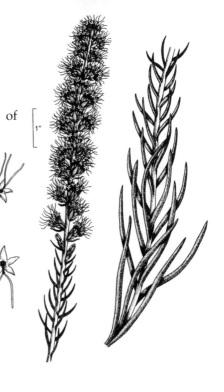

COLOR: Lavender
FLOWERING: Mid-summer to mid-fall
FRUITING: Fall
HEIGHT: 1–5 feet
GROWTH CYCLE: Hardy perennial

Lance-Leaved Coreopsis
Coreopsis lanceolata

The 2-inch daisy-like, yellow flowers are borne on long, smooth, slender stems, making this species an excellent cut flower. The resemblance of the seed to a tick has given this plant one of its common names, tickseed.

COLOR: Yellow
FLOWERING: Late spring to summer
FRUITING: Mid- to late summer
HEIGHT: 8–24 inches
GROWTH CYCLE: Hardy perennial

Linanthus
Linanthus grandiflorus

Linanthus is a strikingly beautiful spring wildflower of the Coastal Ranges in California. The inch-long, trumpet-shaped, silky flowers are white, and tinged with pink or lavender. They appear in dense clusters at the tops of the stems.

COLOR: White with pink or lavender
FLOWERING: Mid-spring to mid-summer
FRUITING: Summer
HEIGHT: 4–20 inches
GROWTH CYCLE: Annual

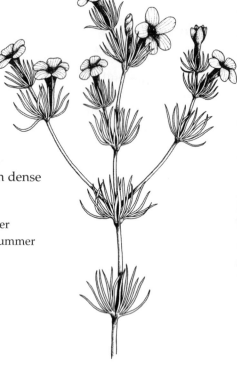

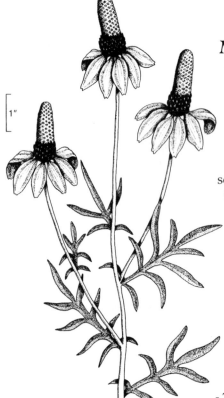

Mexican Hat
Ratibida columnifera

The flowers of this member of the aster family have brown centers protuding ½–2½ inches above the drooping outer petals, giving them the appearance of sombreros. As the dark purple tubular flowers start to bloom from the base of the disc, the hats even appear to have hatbands.

COLOR: Yellow or yellow and red
FLOWERING: Late spring to early fall
FRUITING: Late summer to fall
HEIGHT: 1–3 feet
GROWTH CYCLE: Hardy perennial

New England Aster
Aster novae-angliae

This species is the stock from which many of the horticultural varieties of hardy asters have been bred. Its dense leaves are covered with bristly hairs. The flowers produce ⅛-inch-long fuzzy seeds.

COLOR: Violet-purple with yellow
FLOWERING: Early to mid-fall
FRUITING: Fall
HEIGHT: 1–3 feet
GROWTH CYCLE: Hardy perennial

Pasqueflower
Anemone paten

The solitary, 2–3-inch flowers have 5–7 pointed, petal-like parts which range in color from lavender to pale blue to white. The long plumes of seed-like fruits give rise to one of pasqueflower's other common names, prairie smoke.

COLOR: Lavender to blue to white
FLOWERING: Early spring
FRUITING: Mid- to late spring
HEIGHT: 6–9 inches
GROWTH CYCLE: Hardy perennial

Purple Coneflower
Echinacea purpurea

Though frequently listed in flower seed catalogs around the world, purple coneflower is native to midwestern prairies and dry open woods of the southeastern U.S. It is an excellent cut flower, having long-lasting single flower heads on long stems.

COLOR: Dull purple to crimson
FLOWERING: Late spring to early fall
FRUITING: Fall
HEIGHT: 2–4 feet
GROWTH CYCLE: Hardy perennial

Scarlet Sage
Salvia coccinea

This native of the Southeast should not be confused with *Salvia splendens*, the commonly cultivated scarlet sage which is a native of Brazil. The North American native has all of the color of its South American relative, but lacks its harshness.

COLOR: Scarlet and purple
FLOWERING: Late spring to frost
FRUITING: Summer to fall
HEIGHT: 1–2½ feet
GROWTH CYCLE: Tender perennial that can be grown as an annual in northern gardens

Spiderwort
Tradescantia virginiana

Spiderwort is an old garden favorite which sometmes escapes back into its native habitat, the woods and meadows of the eastern United States. This species can be somewhat invasive, so keep an eye on it and take proper control measures if it starts to crowd out other wildflowers.

COLOR: Light blue to lavender to rose
FLOWERING: Mid-spring to mid-summer
FRUITING: Summer
HEIGHT: 6–18 inches
GROWTH CYCLE: Hardy perennial

Standing Cypress
Ipomopsis rubra

This native of the Southeast and Mexico was once a favorite in northern gardens. It is attractive to both humans and hummingbirds, the latter being the main pollinator of the species. Individual flowers open for 2–5 days, but the overall flowering season is quite long, with a progression of bloom downward from the top of the stem.

COLOR: Scarlet
FLOWERING: Summer
FRUITING: Late summer to early fall
HEIGHT: 3–5 feet
GROWTH CYCLE: Biennial

Tidy Tips
Layia platyglossa

The three-toothed petals of this member of the aster family have white tips and deep yellow bases. While most of the flowers have both colors, some individuals have flowers that are all white or all yellow.

COLOR: White and yellow
FLOWERING: Spring to
  early summer
FRUITING: Summer
HEIGHT: 6–12 inches
GROWTH CYCLE: Annual

Wild Bergamot
Monarda fistulosa

Wild bergamot is a member of the mint family and has the square stems characteristic of that family. Its common name refers to the similarity between the aromas in the pungent foliage of this plant and the fruit of the bergamot orange tree of Europe.

COLOR: Lilac to pink
FLOWERING: Early to mid-summer
FRUITING: Summer to early fall
HEIGHT: 2–4 feet
GROWTH CYCLE: Hardy perennial

Wind Poppy
Stylomecon heterophylla

The wind poppy is native to western California, where its bright blossoms sway in the spring breezes. The 1–2-inch-wide flowers have four broad, silky, vermilion petals with dark purple spots at their bases. Its petals are delicate and fall off easily; therefore it does not make a particularly good cut flower.

1"

COLOR: Red
FLOWERING: Spring
FRUITING: Summer
HEIGHT: 1–2 feet
GROWTH CYCLE: Annual

Books on Wildflowers

Art, H.W., 1986. *A Garden of Wildflowers: 101 Native Species and How to Grow Them.* Garden Way Publishing, Pownal, VT.

Art, H.W., 1987. *The Wildflower Gardener's Guide: Northeast, Mid-Atlantic, Great Lakes, and Eastern Canada Edition.* Garden Way Publishing, Pownal, VT.

Kruckeberg, A.R., 1982. *Gardening with Native Plants of the Pacific Northwest.* U. Washington Press, Seattle, WA.

Martin, Laura C., 1986. *The Wildflower Meadow Book.* East Woods Press, Charlotte, NC.

Phillips, H.R., 1985. *Growing and Propagating Wild Flowers.* U. North Carolina Press, Chapel Hill, NC.

Smith, J.R. & B.S. Smith, 1980. *The Prairie Garden.* U. Wisconsin Press, Madison, WI.

Sperka, M., 1973. *Growing Wildflowers.* Scribner's, New York, NY.

Suppliers

Annie's Annual & Perennials
888-266-4370
www.anniesannuals.com

Brent and Becky's Bulbs
877-661-2852
www.brentandbeckysbulbs.com

Digging Dog Nursery
707-937-1130
www.diggingdog.com

Plant Delights Nursery, Inc.
919-772-4794
www.plantdelights.com

Prairie Nursery
800-476-9453
www.prairienursery.com

Proven Winners
815-895-8130
www.provenwinners.com

Starr Nursery
520-743-7052
www.starr-nursery.com

Timberline Gardens, Inc.
321-735-2279
www.timberlinegardens.com

Other Storey Titles You Will Enjoy

The Complete Guide to Saving Seeds,
by Robert Gough & Cheryl Moore-Gough.
A comprehensive guide to collecting, saving, and cultivating
the seeds of more than 300 vegetables, herbs, and more.

Designer Plant Combinations, by Scott Calhoun.
More than 100 creative combinations by top garden
designers that will inspire home gardeners.

The Flower Gardener's Bible, 2nd edition,
by Lewis and Nancy Hill.
The 10th anniversary edition of the flower gardening classic
that covers everything from planning your garden to caring
for your blooms, and includes a photographic encyclopedia
of over 400 species.

***The Gardener's A–Z Guide to Growing Flowers
from Seed to Bloom,*** by Eileen Powell.
An encyclopedic reference on choosing, sowing, transplanting,
and caring for 576 annuals, perennials, and bulbs.

The Perennial Gardener's Design Primer,
by Stephanie Cohen and Nancy J. Ondra.
A lively, authoritative guide to creating perennial gardens
using basic design principles for putting plants together
in pleasing and practical ways.

Roses Love Garlic, by Louise Riotte.
Secrets to successful companion planting
for hundreds of flowers.

Join the conversation. Share your experience with this book, learn more about
Storey Publishing's authors, and read original essays and book excerpts at storey.com.
Look for our books wherever quality books are sold or by calling 800-441-5700.